STEAM MOTIVE POWER

No.3: DERBY

Including: The Locomotive Works, Engine Shed,
Station & Stabling Points

Copyright Book Law Publications 2008
ISBN 978-1901-945-621

Introduction.

As a railway town, Derby could boast to have been in at the beginning and indeed it was. The place had great traditions and an inevitable pride in its locomotives and rolling stock. Like many great towns in Britain, Derby was built on the banks of a river, the Derwent in this case, but it was the convergence of the railway junctions and the routes radiating in all directions which helped Derby to find a place in railway history. However, the locomotive works, with its adjacent engine sheds, would be the one memory which most enthusiasts could conjure up instantly if asked to do so. The workshops and sheds are now but a memory - they seemed to many of us to be a permanent feature of Derby, a thing that would always be there, no matter what happened - Derby works was needed by British Railways surely.

This album features many aspects of the former LMS railways of Derby in the period spanning the last two decades of steam traction on BR. Besides the locomotive works we have the engine shed, the station, main line and a less palatable feature of Derby which sprang up all around the place - the redundant locomotive storage sites - the dumps.

To present these images we have drawn mainly on the photographs of the late Don Beecroft but Keith Pirt also gets a look-in too with some of his early work capturing the BR which was, up to then, seemingly far from modernisation years which made such an impact on steam traction.

This album is just one of a series which looks at British Railways during the last two decades of steam working. Besides the dedicated albums highlighting the railway towns, we have albums containing heavily illustrated potted line histories for main areas. There are many more either in the pipeline for future publication or already in production.

(*previous page*) **Derby shed Open Day, August 1959. Johnson 3F No.43459 appears to be on its last legs but that was not the case because the 0-6-0 continued in service for another eighteen months.**

Printed and bound by The Amadeus Press, Cleckheaton, West Yorkshire.
First published in the United Kingdom by Book Law Publications, 382 Carlton Hill, Nottingham, NG4 1JA

About to cross over the Five Arches bridge spanning the Derwent, Kentish Town 'Jubilee' No.45616 MALTA G.C. brings a Bradford (Forster Square) - London (St Pancras) express into Derby in August 1959. This train will take the direct route to London via Leicester, heading southwards at Trent. This is another LMS 5XP which spent virtually all of its twenty-six year life working on Midland lines. After an initial allocation to Edge Hill when it came into traffic in September 1934, it moved on to Camden a month later but after helping out with the heavy pre-Christmas traffic from Euston, it changed allegiance to the Midland Division during the following January. Kentish Town were the recipients and it worked from that depot until November 1959 when it transferred to Nottingham. After that it was swapped between Leicester and Trafford Park over the next twelve months but in January 1961 it was withdrawn. No.45616 was only the third of the class to be condemned, the first being the accident damaged No.45637 after the Harrow disaster. No.45609, another Midland lines engines based at Millhouses, was next. Only two more of the class went in 1961, No.45619 from Holbeck and No.45630 from Crewe North. The rot really set in during 1962 when no less than forty-one were condemned.

Passing Derby Junction signal box and starting out over the Five Arches bridge with a freight from Chaddesden yard, ex works Stanier 8F No.48205 heads towards the station and then the Burton line with a running-in turn prior to going home to Toton. The date is June 1957 and steam motive power rules on the main line, admitted many of the yard shunting jobs have been given over to diesel shunters. Derby's prolific production alone has ensured that nearly every engine shed in the country now has an 0-6-0 DE diesel shunter on its books. However, scenes such as this would be repeated for some years to come. After returning to Toton, which had been home since July 1942, the 8F would 'up sticks' after a few weeks and transfer to Hasland. In November 1964, perhaps smelling survival of sorts, No.48205 moved to Lancashire and extended its life by another three years in doing so, first at Bolton then Heaton Mersey. The end came in December 1967, only eight months away from the real end - which wasn't too bad. It was taken to Sheffield for cutting up in March 1968. In the twenty-five years since it was constructed by North British Locomotive Co. in Glasgow, its maker had ceased to exist, its original owner had also gone west and now it too was about to become various metal 'things'. BR had a lot to answer for but at least they knew a thing or two about recycling way back in the fifties.

ly 1958 - the sun is shining on Derby Midland station as Sheffield Millhouses 'Jubilee' No.45590 TRAVANCORE wheels a York-Bristol xpress into platform 4 just after midday. No.45590 was one of the longer-lived members of its class which considering it was a Sheffield ngine was something of an achievement. In December 1961 it transferred to Canklow but two months later it headed west into Lancashire nd ended up at Agecroft where useful work on the Manchester-Fylde coast 'fast' trains ensured a rosier future than its classmates in outh Yorkshire. In June 1963 it crossed Manchester and into the care of Newton Heath who used it for one of the last virtually all steam ummers, although d.m.u.s. had started working some of the longer east-west routes. However, there was never enough diesels to take are of the annual excursion traffic so this 'Jubilee' was fully employed until September. The next episode in No.45590's life saw it move urther west to Warrington Dallam where fitted goods workings kept it going for another two years. However, time was not only running ut for this engine but for steam locomotion in general. Condemned in December 1965, TRAVANCORE was later sold for scrap and took e journey to Great Bridge in March 1966.

Before the BR Standard Cl.2 version of the Ivatt Cl.2 arrived in Derby in 1964, most of the station pilot work was carried out by engine of the latter class, No.46500 being one of them; the others ousted by the BR 2-6-0s were 46402, 46440, 46497, 46499 and 46502. This vie of the 2MT shows it at the south end of Derby station in July 1960 setting back into platform 3. In the adjacent platform is one of th expanding fleet of diesel multiple units which put paid to so many steam locomotives over a very short period from 1956 to 1960. Th signal box (London Road Junction) has is blessed with two pot-bellied stoves and extraordinarily long chimneys. Note the clack valve cove fitted to the Ivatt. On such a small diameter boiler it looks reminiscent of the similar covers used on the WD Stanier 2-8-0s which featur elsewhere n this album.

After its station stop at Derby, the Manchester (Central) - London (St Pancras) express gets underway behind 'Britannia' No.70021 MORNING STAR which is piling on the steam as it sweeps along Spondon curve towards the junction with the Chaddesden line in October 1958. Note that the autumn chill is picking out ant wisp of steam no matter how small. Trafford Park shed would always try to use a 'Brit' on these London turns but they were not always available so 'Scots' and 'Jubilees' would have to suffice. Over the years that the Standard Pacifics worked the Midland Lines expresses, the Manchester depot (actually over the border in Stretford, Lancashire) had a number allocated but could never manage to keep hold of them for long enough before some other depot got the benefit of them. No.70021 arrived at 9E in July 1958 from the Western Region but the engine departed for Willesden in February 1961. No.70004 WILLIAM SHAKESPEARE and No.70014 IRON DUKE were other arrivals in July 1958, courtesy of the Southern Region. Not to be outdone by the SR's generosity, the Western sent No.70015 APOLLO from Cardiff Canton on 12th July. No.70016 ARIEL also joined the throng (which was fast becoming a crowd) at Trafford Park but returned to Cardiff after just a few days. Then came No.70017 ARROW, also courtesy of Canton. In a typical Mancunian expression of exasperation the staff at Trafford Park were heard to say that 'When it rains it pours' meaning of course that after years of struggle something good has come along and lots of it too. Not finished with the WR and SR offerings, the Eastern Region pitched in next on the 19th July with No.70042 LORD ROBERTS. In May 1960 No.70031 BYRON arrived, TENNYSON and CHARLES DICKENS having preceded it by three months. So 1960 proved to be a good year for 9E shed, at least as far as express motive power was concerned but it was not to last, the big diesels were on their way to take over the London trains and from December 1960 the Pacifics were slowly sent away to pastures anew. It had been a short episode for the Trafford Park men but at least they had something decent to drive during that time. In the right background can be seen the lines of stored and derelict steam locomotives waiting on the old carriage sidings at Chaddesden.

Now here is something more like the usual fare handed out for the Manchester-London expresses. Kentish Town 'Jubilee' No.45614 LEEWARD ISLANDS has brought the afternoon St Pancras-Manchester (Central) express to its Derby stop in October 1958. The locomotive looks positively filthy, its numbers difficult to discern properly. Put into traffic at Camden in August 1934 as then un-named No.5614, this engine transferred to Kentish Town five months later and was linked to that depot on and off for the next twenty-six years. Named in 1937, it left London in Match 1940 to spend nearly two months at Toton of all places but returned to 14B in May. It next transfer was not until May 1959 when Newton Heath borrowed it for the summer excursion and Wakes traffic until September when Kentish got it back. Trafford Park had it for a month during February-March 1960 whilst one of their 'Brits', No.70042 was away at Crewe undergoing a Heavy Intermediate overhaul. In December 1961 No.45614 left 14B for good and came to Derby and from the following April Burton had it for nine months when it returned to Derby to undertake its last operational year during which time Derby's shed code was downgraded to 16C. Withdrawal took place in January 1964 after it had been laid off before the previous Christmas. It entered its place of birth in April 1964 and came out in little pieces or was it as bogies for Class 47 diesels? Note the old station buildings which were kept during the 1954 refurbishment of the station, the line of the original overall roof is quite prominent below the windows of the first floor.

Another express calling at Derby during that October 1958 afternoon was this Bristol (Temple Meads)-Newcastle (Central) express. Although its exterior appearance is filth (the order of the day) 'Jubilee' No.45651 SHOVELL seems to be in good form as it restarts the train on its northbound journey. No.45651 was one of the Bristol Barrow Road stud and had worked this train through from Bristol and which it will take on to York. For its first five years this engine was allocated to various LMS Western Division depots but in December 1939 it moved over to the Midland Division at Holbeck. It left Leeds in April 1953 for Barrow Road where it was to be a regular performer on trains such as this for the next eight years. In September 1961 it moved to Saltley and was an early candidate for withdrawal in November 1962. It too was another Crewe built engine which migrated back to darkest Cheshire. The water column on the right has a feature not often seen as the circumstances for its fitting were quite rare. Between the bag and the cast iron column is a moveable bracket which extends horizontally when the 'bag' is in use and, as can be seen, tucks away nicely when not. It was found to be necessary to hold the 'bag' in the horizontal position because the excessive span would cause the weight of water coursing through into the tender to otherwise pull it out of the filler hole. I wonder if that was a manufacturers idea or a local invention?

9

Derby station was blessed with an Up and Down set of goods bypass lines situated to the east of the station. In August 1964 Stanier Class 5 No.45088 is taking advantage of the easy and uncongested Down side track en route to Chaddesden sidings to pick up its train. In the distance can be seen an 8F heading a goods the wrong way i.e. northwards along the Up line. One can only assume a two-way working was in operation on the goods lines. To the left of the 8F, immediately behind the Engine Siding No.1 signal box, can be seen another 8F shunting in the works precinct. This footpath alongside the main line offered a superb vantage point to observe trains passing through Derby but a lot of the goods trains bound for Trent junction from the north would turn off the main line at Derby North junction and pass through the Chaddesden group of sidings to Spondon junction. The Midland Pullman used that same route during its six years of operation from 1960 to 1966, never passing through Derby station during that time. According to the signal gantry the place is fairly quiet but we can observe three different movements from here, with only one signal showing as off.

Schoolboys line up on the platform opposite London Road Junction signal box as 'Jubilee' No.45651 SHOVELL slowly gets a York-Bristol express on the move in July 1960. Typical of the Bristol Barrow Road 'Jubilees', the engine is filthy and would end up being an early candidate for withdrawal in November 1962, a year when no less than forty-one of the class were condemned. Initially allocated to Bushbury shed in January 1935, this engine was transferred to numerous depots the length and breadth of the old LMS Western Division over the next four years, Aston, Camden, Crewe North, Edge Hill, Patricroft, Preston and Upperby all using it for various periods of time. In December 1939 it moved over to the Midland Division at Holbeck and spent nearly fourteen years there before moving to Bristol in April 1953. With the end in sight, No.45651 transferred to Shrewsbury in September 1961 but by then its was worn out and ready for the chop.

11

Sneaking through the goods lines at Midland station that July in 1960 was this local 3F 0-6-0 No.43459 on a short freight train, the origins and destination of which were not logged but the journey would not have been too prolonged either way as the Johnson 0-6-0s were no longer being entrusted with anything of importance by this date. This engine had been at Derby since at least WW2 prior to which it had been at Nottingham so it was always a bit of a local lad around this part of the old Midland. One of sixty such engines supplied to the Midland by Dubs & Co. in 1892-93, it was rebuilt by both Deeley and Fowler during the first two decades of the twentieth century. The end came swiftly. Withdrawal took place in April 1961, it was whisked off to Crewe in May and promptly cut up.

Don Beecroft's notes for this picture simply say: '42587 shunting Derby (Midland) July 1960'. However, the engine's headlamp code is showing Ordinary Passenger Train, Mixed Train, Branch Passenger Train, etc. Also, the carriages behind the parcels van (a bit of a mixed bunch) are occupied by a number of people judging by how many are at the windows. So was this a main line working or a shunting movement? The Stanier 2-6-4T was, in July 1960 at least, allocated to 17A Derby having transferred from St Albans during the previous February, so nothing unusual there. It would be interesting to know why this train was being shunted. Was it being added to another already in a platform? Or being taken off one which had just arrived from some unknown and far off station? One thing for certain, nowadays we just do not witness this kind of station activity. Everything is in unit form going from A to B, stopping en route but never dropping stock off or picking it up. It is pretty sterile and therefore not as interesting as those heady days of the steam era.

13

Seen from the Five Arches bridge parapet, the 5-05 p.m. local to Bakewell, headed by Stanier Class 5 No.44851, leaves Derby (Midland) on a sunny August evening in 1964. The locomotive works is on the left and the signal box control the north end of the station is framed beneath the huge signal gantry which dominated the scene. The 4-6-0 was one of the Crewe built examples and came into traffic during November 1944. Although it does not appear so here, with its atrocious external condition, No.44851 was one of the class which survived into 1968. Its first shed was Derby where it was to spent the next nine years prior to transferring to Millhouses, the two month loan to Polmadie from July to September 1953 not only took it out of division but also out of region and out of the country! In October 1955 it returned to Derby for a seven year bash after which it was allocated to Burton for just a month before moving over to Nottingham in October 1962. In March 1963 it returned to Burton but a month later it went back to Nottingham as though on a piece of elastic. In September 1964 Burton got it back and held on to the Cl.5 until March 1966 when the Northwest and survival beckoned. Trafford Park was its first shed in Lancashire, hardly one of the best places to go but two more years of operation was secured. The start of the end came in March 1968 with a transfer to Newton Heath but only weeks later No.44851 was condemned. Newton Heath was crammed with Stanier engines but they were no longer required. In June the 4-6-0 left 9D and was towed to a scrap merchant in Kettering.

14

July 1960 - Thompson B1's were rare at Birmingham (New Street) station, even in the heady days of the early sixties, so this one will cause some excitement when it arrives later in the afternoon. No.61312 is heading a Sheffield (Midland)-Birmingham express which is made up from BR Mk.1 coaches. At this time the B1 was allocated to the ex Midland shed at Canklow and was engaged mainly on goods workings of all types including hauling slow, lumbering and heavy mineral trains. No doubt the discoloration and distortion on the bottom of the smokebox door has been caused by hard work at slow speed rather than running at high speed. No.61312 had spent about half of its life so far working on the former Great Eastern lines, being transferred from Darnall to Norwich in October 1954. It returned to Sheffield in May 1959 after a spell at Yarmouth too. Staveley Central shed had it for three months in late 1959 prior to its Canklow transfer. Darnall would get it again in September 1961 but after a year there it moved once more to Staveley. King's Cross was its home from March to June 1963 when Mexborough took it in. Strangely, this 4-6-0 underwent General overhauls at all four former LNER workshops in England during its sixteen year life; Gorton and Stratford undertook two 'Generals' each whilst Darlington and Doncaster each performed one such overhaul. Withdrawn 1st March 1964, it was sold for scrap in May and cut up in Rotherham.

15

The Derby (Midland) station pilot in August 1964 was BR Standard Cl.2 No.78000 which is seen here heading north out of the station with a padlocked S&CM Department stores van. The BR Standard classes offered untold comforts to enginemen, especially those used to working the Midland engines with their open cabs. But they came too late, or rather the Modernisation Plan came too soon so that the full impact of the Standards could not be ascertained, appreciated or utilised. The angular lines of the 78000 Class especially seem to have leanings to designs across the Atlantic. At least they appeared to carry the dirt and filth much more easily than the pre-Group and Big Four designs did. In the background is Derby Junction signal box which controlled the lines coming from Chaddesden sidings and the alternative route to the east through Spondon junction, besides the main line from the north. Just to the right of the signal box and making its way towards the station light engine, can be seen the carriage pilot for the day, another Cl.2 No.78020.

In August 1964 'Jubilee' No.45611 HONG KONG retained its nameplates but not its shedplate. Its home depot was Derby which had recently (September 1963) switched from being 17A to 16C and new plates would have to be made but it seems none ever were. If the last depot with the 16C code, Mansfield, kept their plates then there would not have been enough to hand round anyway at Derby because Mansfield's meagre stud stood at not more than a dozen engines when the depot closed, not enough to fix to a sixth of Derby's lot. The filthy 'Jubilee' is heading a parcels train to Manchester, one of the few jobs it undertook before withdrawal in September. This engine had long been a favourite at Nottingham where it spent more than twelve years before moving to Burton in November 1961. When No.45611 transferred to Derby in January 1963 the 4-6-0 was already regarded as a 'cast-off', its external condition being far from favourable. Like so many of its kind at that time it was merely used until something drastic, or minor, went wrong and when it did - condemnation. The 'Jubilee' was sold for scrap to Cashmores at Great Bridge in January 1965 after lying derelict at the shed since September.

No.78020 stops on the Five Arches bridge to await its next job. When these Standard 2-6-0s first came to Derby, Nos.78000 and 78021 arrived in January 1964, they worked the Shirland Colliery branch which was situated to the north between Ambergate and Clay Cross. They took over that job from three ageing Johnson 0-6-0 3F tender engines but the colliery, then producing in excess of 200,000 tons of coal a year, was in decline and production ceased during the following year. In May 1964 five further Standard Cl.2 transferred from Wigan, Nos.78020, 78027, 78037, 78057 and 78061, but these came in exchange for five Ivatt Cl.2 which moved to Springs Branch. Over the following twelve months Derby lost some of their seven Cl.2 to places like Leicester and Lostock Hall although 78064 came from the former L&Y depot at Wigan Central. By April 1965 only three of the 2-6-0s remained at Derby - 78000 (1st in class), 78020 (depicted here) and 78064 (last of class). In June 1965 the Class leader was withdrawn whilst the other two got on with pilot jobs like this. In October 1966 the surviving pair transferred to Toton of all places, where they were immediately put into store. In November 1966 No.78020 transferred to Lostock Hall and managed to eke out a further six months of work before the scrapman finally caught up with it in May 1967. No.78064 was condemned whilst in the storage line at Toton in November 1966 - it was aged exactly ten years.

The former LNWR and NSR goods depot at St Andrews was surplus to requirements by early 1959 and so the empty yard became a convenient place to dump redundant locomotives. The yard was situated immediately south and west of Derby (Midland) station and was in sight of the main lines to both Trent and Burton, although from the latter route a better view of the contents of the yard could be had. To placate those who glanced into the yard from a passing train but never had the chance of entering the place we are going to undertake a quick photographic survey of the residents in May 1959. On one of the dead-end sidings were two Compounds, Nos.41102 and 41090, both of LMS origin and totally intact and they had each been withdrawn in the previous December. No.41090 had been shedded at Monument Lane until June 1958 when it transferred to Derby. No.41102 on the other hand had been much more active trying to find a permanent home during the fifties and although staying within the boundaries of Lancashire, it nevertheless managed to have six different homes during the eight year period from January 1950 to withdrawal. The list leads one to believe that this 4-4-0 enjoyed the seaside, football and horse racing: Southport three times; Wigan Central; Walton-on-the-Hill; Aintree; Lancaster; Blackpool twice. It was from the latter shed that this engine made its final journey to Derby, at first on transfer to 17A before ending up in this temporary dump. For the record, No.41090 had been built here in Derby in 1925 whilst No.41102 had its roots in Lancashire being built in 1927 at Vulcan Foundry in Newton-le-Willows - old habits die hard. One of its first postings was Newton Heath from where trips to the coast became an everyday occurrence. After languishing in this yard for another year, both engines were towed to Doncaster for cutting up in June 1960.   19

A list of the inhabitants of St Andrews goods yard reads like a Midland Railway engine design catalogue and Johnson 2P No.40413 was typical of what was to be found there. Intact except for a shedplate, the 4-4-0 had been condemned in January 1959 after arriving at derby from Kentish Town, its home for the last eighteen months of its operational existence. Prior to that it had spent five years at Crewe North shed, having a liking for the former LMS Western Division depots. Way back in 1935 for instance it was allocated to Buxton whilst at Nationalisation it was resident at Walsall. Prior to the 5A transfer it was at Nuneaton and then Stafford. Built in 1892 by Sharp Stewart & Co., this engine had undergone a certain amount of rebuilding under Deeley in MR days and later by Fowler in the early LMS years. However, No.40413 could claim to be sixty-eight years old when it was eventually towed the short distance to Looms yard at Spondon in early 1960. In the immediate background is Deeley 3F 0-6-0 No.43771 which was withdrawn during the previous February but was to rot here for two years before being hauled away for scrapping at Looms in February 1961. It may be of interest to rolling stock enthusiasts and modellers to know that the 16-ton mineral wagon standing alongside the 0-6-0 had two legends painted on its side sheets. The one within the black painted square on the left read TO WORK BETWEEN DENBY COLLIERY B.E.A. SPONDON L.M.R. 16T. The white painted message on the right hand side is much more interesting and reads: AXLEBOX TEE BOLTS ON TRIAL NOT TO BE DISTURBED WITHOUT APPROVAL C/W ENGINEER L.M.REGION. It is not certain why this wagon was in the yard, perhaps it was dumped or had been supplied so that someone could empty the contents of the tenders. From this vantage point it is just possible to see the roof of London Road Junction signal box on the extreme right, its two tall metal chimneys being distinctive.

As mentioned earlier in this piece featuring the inhabitants of St Andrews yard, it was distinctly Midland in there which, in a place like Derby was not hard to find. The only tank engine stored there in May 1959 was this former Midland Johnson Goods Tank which was built at Vulcan Foundry in June 1902 as MR No.2770. It started its working life at Trafford Park shed on the Cheshire Lines and was renumbered 1949 as part of the Midland 1907 renumbering scheme. By the start of the Great war it was resident at Kentish Town along with Nos.1940 to 1951. Between 1924 and 1928 the LMS fitted eleven members of the class with condensing apparatus and No.1949 was so fitted in October 1925, which then enabled it to work goods traffic over the Metropolitan widened lines to destinations in south-east London. Thirty of the class had been fitted with condensing apparatus at building and these engines were concentrated at Cricklewood shed initially but Kentish Town shed was also able to share this lucrative traffic hence the reason for equipping its stud in the twenties. At the end of 1935 No.1949 was still allocated to Kentish Town but during WW2, now numbered 7249, it transferred away from London to Saltley. By Nationalisation it was resident at Toton but shortly afterwards it moved further north to Stourton. In December 1957 it was sent to its final shed which came about to be Sowerby Bridge, a somewhat strange transfer considered. That move lasted just nine months before it came to Derby for consideration. As you can see the inevitable happened and, still fitted with the condensing apparatus, No.47249 ended up at St Andrews prior to being dragged to Doncaster works for scrapping in March 1960.

This picture of LMS Compound No.41113, at St Andrews in May 1959, has been included to show the steam pipe for the inside cylinder is fitted to the right side of the smokebox whilst on other engines of this class it was positioned on the left side (see No.41059 on Derby shed). No.41113 was built in November 1925 at Derby when these engines were regarded, by many, as the 'top link' LMS express passenger locomotives. Indeed their strategic allocation throughout the LMS system saw that the class of 195 engines was well placed to serve most of the important passenger services of the day. The bulk of the class was delivered by July 1927 but after a five year delay five further Compounds were built at Derby in 1932 before Stanier blocked an order requiring another twenty 4-4-0s. In 1935, as No.1113, this 4-4-0 was allocated to Monument Lane shed, an ex LNWR establishment where, along with other sheds of the same ilk, these compounds were regarded with some unease. Allowed to run on the main line at high speeds they were good when handled properly but if badly handled on unsuitable work they were next to useless - like a greyhound pulling a sled up and downhill. By the time BR came into being No.41113 had moved to Longsight and then in July 1952 to Rugby. Its final depot was Lancaster where it got some sympathy on arrival there in May 1958 but its time was up and in December it was condemned. This engine was sold for scrap in February 1960 and ended up in Cashmores yard at Great Bridge. Note the lack of a works plate.

Goods engines were a bit thin on the ground at St Andrews in May 1959 and only three were recorded, one already mentioned, No.43771, 58192 and this other Johnson 2F 0-6-0 No.58225. This was a Beyer, Peacock model from February 1884, another old-timer. Renumbered in October 1948 from its LMS No.3118, it was withdrawn in December 1958. Its last shed under the LMS regime was Grimesthorpe, prior to which it had worked in the somewhat greener surroundings at Rowsley. It was to stay at the Sheffield depot until withdrawal and note that it still wears the 19A shedplate some ten months after Grimesthorpe became part of the Eastern Region and its code was changed to 41B. It was eventually despatched to Crewe works for cutting up nearly two years after withdrawal.

23

St Andrews goods yard continued.(*above*) Compound No.41083, minus connecting rod but still has a works plate attached. Note that the inside cylinder steam pipe is on the right side. (*below*) Johnson 2F No.58192. Note the 19A Grimesthorpe shedplate. The 0-6-0 was sent to Doncaster for scrapping in March 1960. The 4-4-0 went to the private yard at Great Bridge a few weeks previously. Other locomotives at this yard included Nos.40553, 41173, 43180, 43244, 43274, 43357, 43578, 43612, 43712, 43787. Besides this dump there was one alongside the West main line, another at Way & Works sidings, one opposite the station, the timber sidings near Spondon junction, whilst the dump at Chaddesden shall have our attention later.

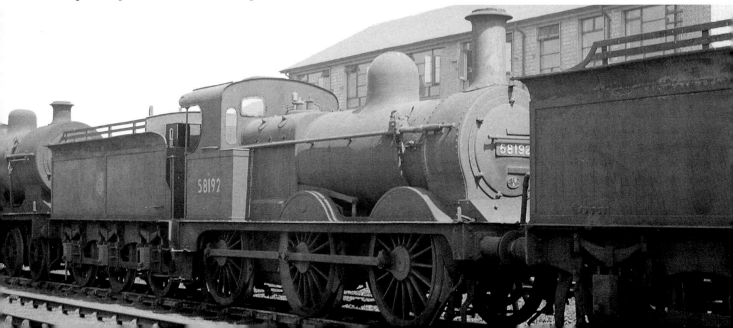

W.G.Bagnall of Stafford did not make that many locomotives for the main lines railways compared to their industrial and overseas customers. However, the LMS purchased thirty-one 3F 0-6-0T 'Jinties' from them in four separate lots during the period from 1926 to 1929 - i.e. eight, Nos.7452-7460 in 1926; six, Nos.7461-7466 in 1927; ten, 7592-7601 in 1928; seven, 7310-7316 from December 1928 to February 1929 (note that the later LMS numbers have been used rather than the initial four and five digit numbers used up to 1934. In the case of Nos.7310-7316, these never carried the five digit number and started life, at least in the Order book, as Somerset & Dorset Joint Committee Nos.19-25, WGB Nos.2358-2364 of 1929. They came into traffic as LMS Nos.7150-7156, becoming 7310-7316 in the 1934 renumbering scheme). No.47315, seen here in Derby during August 1959, had spent virtually the whole of its life working from Devons Road shed in east London and only moved from there to Willesden in March 1958 because Devons Road was being refurbished to become Britain's first all purpose diesel depot. The former North London Railway locomotive works at Bow used to take care of its every need in the maintenance department but when their charges got beyond economic repair they sent them up to Derby for decision. On arrival at Derby in August 1959 the 0-6-0T was immediately condemned, Willesden shed hardly using it for any purpose since it arrived there eighteen months previously. Besides the need for a new boiler, the engine had some accident damage that was not considered worth repairing. It was cut up at Derby in September. Note that No.47315 is not carrying a works plate. Where did all those Bagnall plates go?   25

In June 1955, Barrow Hill based Johnson 1F 0-6-0T No.41749 entered the precincts of Derby works for the last time, the seventy-one year old veteran was finished and within days would be cut up. Note the boilers waiting to be either repaired, re-used or, most probably scrapped. The unidentified Fowler 2-6-2T behind No.41749 is in no danger yet of being condemned, the first of that class was not withdrawn until 1959 when more than half of its class disappeared during the year.

(*opposite*) One of the smallest ex MR engines was No.41516, the 0F 0-4-0ST designed in the Johnson era and built at Derby in March 1897. At just twenty-three tons, wet through, this engine was even smaller than the Deeley 0F tank just described and which weighed in at a 'massive' thirty-two tons. This locomotive has obviously been an inspiration to television producers and cartoon designers over the years but in October 1955, when it was photographed at Derby works, there was nothing funny about its forthcoming predicament because it was in for a special examination. It was also there to have an official photograph taken in BR livery before the inevitable occurred. The new 'livery' had apparently only just been applied and although difficult to discern in this photograph, the engine is in fact painted grey for the camera. The right side of the engine was unpainted and the tank still carried the legend LMS. Needless to say the 0-4-0ST failed its exam and was condemned. Originally there had been thirty such engines in this class which had been introduced in 1883 with their construction carried out in small batches up to 1903. When BR came into being only four of the original engines survived and one of those (No.1509) succumbed in October 1949 without having its BR number applied No.41516 nearly went the same way. Two more, Nos.41518 and 41523, were from the late 1897 and 1903 batches respectfully and had been built with longer wheelbases, larger cylinders and greater water capacity so therefore weighed nine tons more than No.41516 - the only true survivor which also retained its open back cab. This engine and No.41523 were both allocated to Burton-on-Trent shed and worked the brewery lines around that town but No.41523 had already been consigned to scrap in March 1955 and so only two were left. No.41518 worked at Hasland up to April 1955 but then moved to Barrow Hill to take up work alongside the Deeley 0-4-0Ts in Staveley works. The tenderless 0-6-0 in the rear is No.58306, a Johnson 2F which was in for repair and was returned to traffic.

Whenever 'Big Bertha' aka No.58100 visited Derby works for a major overhaul it did not usually take long to complete because the locomotive had a spare boiler which was ready in time for each visit. However, the cylinder block with its four cylinders was unique so any major work required on that would have held up the overhaul but everything seems to be right on Sunday 31st May 1953 with the front end of the locomotive touched up with black paint. In this view we can easily see the front sanding box below the cylinder and, beneath the cab, the generator for the headlight. It returned to Bromsgrove without any incident.

(*opposite*) Two years have passed since we last saw 'Big Bertha' after the 'General' in November 1954 and now the big 0-10-0 it has returned to its birthplace for the last time. It has been condemned and will no longer run on the main line. Note that the headlight and associated generator have been removed, BR Standard 9F No.92079 now wears them and apparently it was shaping up to the banking job like a natural. The big old lady here will linger on for a while yet. As a start was made to scrap the engine, it was partly dismantled just before the works 1956 open day but somebody on the staff had the bright idea of letting the crowds see the engine in all its glory so, it was hurriedly put back together for the crowds to admire. But that was just a reprieve to the inevitable which did not fully take place until April 1957 when the cylinder block was cut up. The power station forms the background to this rather sad scene.

Five Stanier 8F 2-8-0s belonging to the War Department were overhauled at Derby works during the period from July 1952 to late 1954. Having arrived from the Middle East at Birkenhead aboard the S.S.Ben Ledi, the five 2-8-0s were devoid of tenders, and other parts, so tenders had to be borrowed for the tow to Derby. Their stay at the works was somewhat protracted and was to last over two years with conversion to oil burning also being part of their rehabilitation and overhaul. This line-up in the works yard on 28th November 1954 has WD Nos.508, 511 and 512 stored awaiting tenders. The tenders, which were still in Suez, were about to be loaded aboard the S.S. Benvannock for arrival at London docks in early 1955. The two painted engines in this view (508 and 511) eventually ended up at Cairn Ryan Military Port near Stranraer but did little or no work there, both being cut up in 1959. Note that No.512 is missing certain parts but it does have a normal sized clack valve cover compared to the rather large appendages on the other two engines. WD 501 was also about the works and was apparently being made ready to undergo trials. The last mentioned engine and WD 512 did of course become British Railways property in September 1957 when they entered service as 48774 and 48775 respectively. The third member of that batch, 48773 (WD 500) was not amongst those present at Derby on this date having already been overhauled and returned to the Army at Longmoor. The three 'repatriated' BR engines all went to Polmadie depot but returned to England in 1963 via Kingmoor. From there they moved on and split up going to Stockport Edgeley, Speke Junction and Buxton respectively. No.48773 has, of course, been preserved. K.R.Pirt.

As already mentioned, the LMS Fowler 2-6-2T 3MT class was devastated in 1959 when half of the seventy locomotives were condemned. This is No.40047 in late August 1959 being slowly stripped in the Klondyke. It was finally withdrawn in November but it was not cut up by Derby until January 1960 - a protracted affair which was repeated many times in this period. Derby once had a reputation for cutting up locomotives before their condemnation was officially reported and it is a fact that a number of engines were withdrawn after they had ceased to exist! No.40047 was a member of a class which, from day one in March 1930, had a bad reputation. They were underboilered (the usual Derby problem) and had a tortuous path for both live and exhaust steam. The later steam problem was later rectified on some of the class but the boiler problem remained. It is amazing that the railway managed to get thirty years life out of them although they never did get thirty years work out of them. This engine arrived from Willesden shed which had tried to get rid of it to Wolverton carriage works in February 1958 but less than a month later it was returned to 1A as not required, it was after all a Derby product with MR stamped all over the design.

31

In May 1956 Derby contained in its quest to push out more 350 h.p. 0-6-0 diesel-electric shunters than any other workshop or private manufacturer. Having let up for a one month break in March to put 13213 to 13216 into traffic, the works started producing the diesel again in May with 13245-13249 being built. That five unit production run is seen here with 13247 heading the line and waiting to enter traffic - 16A Nottingham being the case along with 13246; 13245 went to Crewe south whilst the other two stayed in the parish, allocated to 17A. In June Derby built twelve of these locomotives which were eventually to become TOPS Class 08. No.13247 became D3247 in March 1961 then in August 1974 it was renumbered 08179 only to be withdrawn less than a year later. It was broken up at Swindon works which then vied with the surviving BR workshops and private scrap yards to see who could put the most 08's to the torch. It is something of an irony that Derby was still building steam locomotives whilst all this diesel construction was taking place, likewise steam locomotives were being broken up on the premises as was the occasional diesel locomotive.

Even when the new BR emblem was being applied Derby was still turning out the diesel shunters with the 1 prefix. as to 13365 in June 1957 but that was soon to change because later that month D3358 came out of the shops with the D prefix. The last one to have the 1 applied was 13366, also in June. Note that Derby was not building their batches in strict numerical order. The batch 13337 to 13357 were turned out between March and June 1957 whilst 13363 to 13365 came out May to June. D3358 to D3362 came out June to August 1957 (annual holidays in there somewhere) whilst D3367 to D3418 picked up the thread from July onwards. For the record 13365 became D3365 in April 1963 and 08295 in February 1974. It started work in South Wales at Cardiff East Dock but ended up at Thornaby where in May 1988 it was withdrawn. Note that the lion on the new BR emblem is in fact facing the wrong way, a mistake BR had to put right eventually.

Jackshaft drive diesel shunter No.12025 was an ex LMS locomotive built at Derby in the dark days of February 1942. It was part of a continuous line of diesel shunters constructed by the London Midland & Scottish Railway at Derby from May 1939 until July 1942 when wartime constraints halted the production line. The line started up again in April 1945 when the Allied Victory was basically assured. From that day on Derby continued to build diesel locomotives until 1967 when the line was finished for good. This locomotive started life at Kingmoor shed along with five others of its kind numbered 7110 to 7115. No.12025 carried the number 7112 until May 1952 when it was renumbered at Derby works shortly before it was caught on film within the premises. The end came in December 1967 at Speke Junction its last depot. It was sold for scrap to Slag Reduction at Rotherham and cut up in October 1968.

They were quite ugly really the two LMS main line Co-Co diesel locomotives. Although based, after a fashion, and quite loosely, on the United States model, the British equivalent did not have the height or clean sweeping lines of the Union Pacific or Santa Fe 'F' units. Still, even more ugly was to come from the British Railways stable and its various contractors during the next decade and a half so the LMS did a reasonable job really considering austerity and other post-war problems. This is the second of the twins, No.10001, at Derby (I'm not sure where) in February 1956. Now before I drop myself in it I must point out that this particular unit did not come into traffic until July 1948 so was actually a BR model. Both locomotives were however built at Derby works and would often return for periods of testing, storage or to undertake some modification, no matter how small. In late 1956 BR standard green livery was applied to these locomotives but here it still has the black body and silver painted bogies. Neither of the pair was preserved, or even considered for such which, in the circumstances seems a poor show as they were Britain's first main line diesel locomotives. Milestones in transport !!!

By the end of October 1953 Derby works had turned out forty-three of the BR Standard Class 5 4-6-0 since putting No.73000 into traffic in April 1951. This is No.73042 on Sunday 25th October 1953 with its first tenderful of coal waiting to have its first fire lit ready for initial testing. This is a nice piece of kit for a £19,974 showroom price tag but it was still £2,371 more expensive than each of the 1951 batch but post-war inflation was marching on. This was the third engine of a batch of ten built for the London Midland Region (73040-73049), the last of which entered traffic immediately after the New Year. Chester (exLNWR) was its initial shed to which Nos.73040 and 73041 had also been allocated. They were not the first new Standard Cl.5 to be sent to 6A, because exactly two years previously, in October 1951, Nos.73020 to 73022 were sent there. Chester shed appears to have receive these new engine in batches of three at a time because in November 1954 Nos.73070 to 73072 were also sent there. Less than five years were to pass before No.73042 was transferred to the Southern Region at Stewarts Lane depot, No.73041 was sent along too and the two 4-6-0s settled down to a new life pulling green carriage stock. Both engines were withdrawn fairly early on compared with their named SR counterparts, No.73041 in June 1965 whilst 73042 followed in August. The Standard is 'top and tailed' in this view by two other ex works locomotives, Fowler 2-6-4T No.42361 of Nottingham shed and 'Jinty' No.47670 from Crewe South. K.R.Pirt.

(*opposite*) We move on now to May 1955 when the Standard Cl.5 4-6-0 building programme still had nearly two years to go as far as Derby was concerned. By now a batch of five for the Scottish Region (73075-73079) were starting to enter traffic and No.73077 is ready for its journey to Eastfield shed. Note that this engine is coupled to a BR1C type tender with flush sides and weighing over four tons heavier, at 53ù tons, than the BR1 attached to No.73042. This Class 5 was to have a short life of just nine years, being condemned in December 1964 at Corkerhill depot.

Another ex works Standard on Derby shed in 1953 was No.75011, one of the Cl.4 versions of 4-6-0 which started to appear from Swindon works at the same time that Derby was bringing out the Cl.5. Allocated to Patricroft shed at this time, August, this engine has just had a tender change which appears to have new draught excluders fitted and has received a repaint in the process. The engine has gone through a cursory clean which included just the smokebox whilst the cabside number has also been given the cloth treatment. From this view, taken from a Nottingham bound train, we can see the outdoor turntable with numerous engines grouped around its perimeter. It was always frustrating when passing an engine shed to which a visit was not planned, to see so many locomotives yet be unable to record their numbers. Outside turntables with multiple stabling roads were not usual in Britain, unlike continental Europe and the United States, but Derby was blessed with this one from about 1900 as part of a scheme to build another 'roundhouse', offset slightly to the No.4 shed which itself was completed in 1890. The fifth shed was never built but the turntable and its sixteen radiating roads remained in use until 1963 when an incident with a tank locomotive caused a great deal of damage to the by now 70ft table which led to its premature demise some four years before the depot closed. No.75011 outlived the turntable but not the depot as it was withdrawn from Skipton shed in November 1966. Incidentally this 4-6-0 was allocated to 17A Derby from May to November 1963.

Visiting Saltley Stanier Cl.5 No.44814 is seen stabled off the outside turntable in May 1956 whilst in the background resident Ivatt Cl.4 No.43041 is stabled on one of the straight roads which ran parallel to the main shed. An unidentified 'Jubilee' can be seen on the extreme right. No.44814 went new to Saltley in October 1944 and was to spend twenty years at that depot before transferring to Rugby in April 1964. Later it went to Woodford Halse but moved to Holyhead in June 1965 and then, three months later to Shrewsbury. Finally, in March 1967, it went to Crewe South for a six month stint before it was withdrawn. The 2-6-0 was one of the rare London Midland based examples of its class which managed to stay firmly allocated within the region. Its final transfer took it to Lostock Hall in February 1966 and it was there that it was condemned in August 1967.

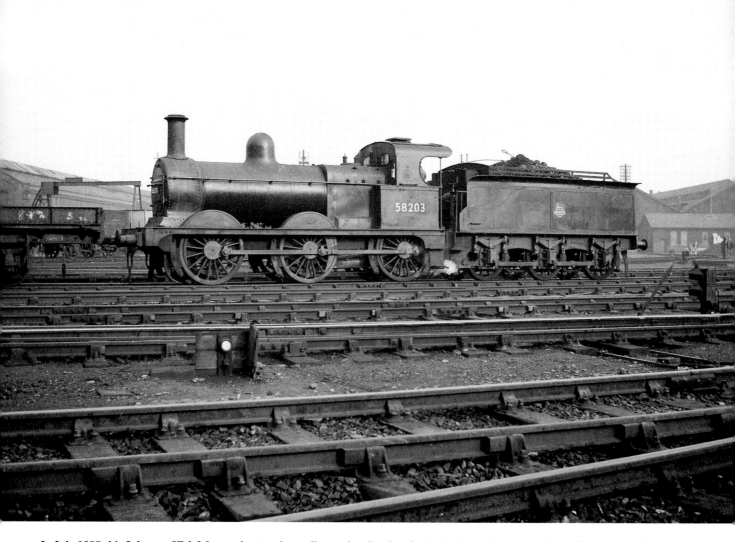

In July 1955 this Johnson 2F 0-6-0 was about to be reallocated to Patricroft shed after a three year stint at Shrewsbury 84G depot. It was at Derby works for an Intermediate overhaul and, that finished, is ready to make its way to Manchester. It was not long at 10C and by the following February had taken up residence at Springs Branch shed in Wigan but that was a short-lived stay because in March 1956 it moved on to Walsall shed from where it ended its days in January 1958. Considering this engine was of pure Midland origin, its last four sheds were anything but, all of them being of LNWR origin. Built in January 1880, it was one of a batch supplied to the Midland Railway by Robert Stephenson & Co. Originally having a round topped firebox, it was rebuilt with this larger Belpaire boiler, larger cylinders and wheels. Numbered 3054 by the LMS, the veteran was renumbered 58203 by British Railways in August 1948. Already seventy-five years old when this photograph was captured, the 0-6-0 was certainly on borrowed time, its services not really required. It entered Derby works for the last time in January 1958 and, after a few months waiting for a decision to sell or scrap, it was broken up in March.

Another visitor on Derby shed in May 1956 was ex works Stanier 8F No.48618 which had just completed a 'General' and was looking resplendent in its new coat of shiny black paint. The Toton based 2-8-0 was another which ended its days at Lostock Hall in 1967, being condemned in September of that year. No.48618 was one of the Southern Railway built examples which after completion at Ashford in September 1943 was sent to work on the LMS at Holbeck. A year later Toton acquired it and managed to hold on to it for fourteen years. It went, on loan, to Barrow Hill in July 1958 but they then kept it until May 1963 when it moved over to Lancashire for an extension of life at Newton Heath. Fleetwood had its services from March 1964 until June 1965 when Lostock Hall called.

Although Derby shed did not have many of the glamorous 'namers' allocated at any one time during BR days, a surprising number of them had been allocated to the shed during the last thirty years of steam. Some sixty-four 'Jubilees' had passed through, some staying a few weeks, others for a few years whilst others had two and more residencies at 17A, one, No.45602 had six separate stints. Five 'Royal Scots' came and went during the latter years, especially when the West Coast main line had no further use for them. One of them, No.46120 was allocated no less than seven times. The Fowler parallel boiler 'Patriots' were somewhat thin on the ground at 17A but one particular and very appropriate engine, No.45509 THE DERBYSHIRE YEOMANRY, was allocated after being named in October 1951. It then resided for the next seven years until moving on to Newton Heath in the summer of 1958. Here, in February 1956, it has just completed servicing at Derby and is stabled on one of the outside turntable radiating roads.

Open Days at Derby works and shed became an annual summer event with clean and polished visiting locomotives set out for photography within the works yard. More than likely something special would turn up that had no link with the workshops - a Crewe product which was usually a Pacific. The shed visit on those days, for most enthusiasts, was the icing on the cake where the rare stuff might be hiding. In August 1959 the sun shone all day for the 'do' and everyone enjoyed themselves. Caprotti fitted Standard Class 5 No.73141 was neither rare nor polished, it was not part of the exhibition itinerary and had been dumped at the side of the shed awaiting attention from fitters to the area around the smokebox. It was a 17A engine and had been since the previous January when Leicester Midland shed let it go. It was not yet three years old but was looking rather run down. According to official figures it had not yet run enough miles to warrant a boiler change but it was probably due for an Intermediate overhaul. Amongst the last batch of Derby built steam locomotives, No.73141 was turned out in December 1956 and had cost £28,075 to build, somewhat more expensive than the non-Caprotti Cl.5. This engine ended its days at Patricroft shed like most of the LM Region Standard 5s' and was withdrawn in July 1967, barely ten years old - some depreciation.

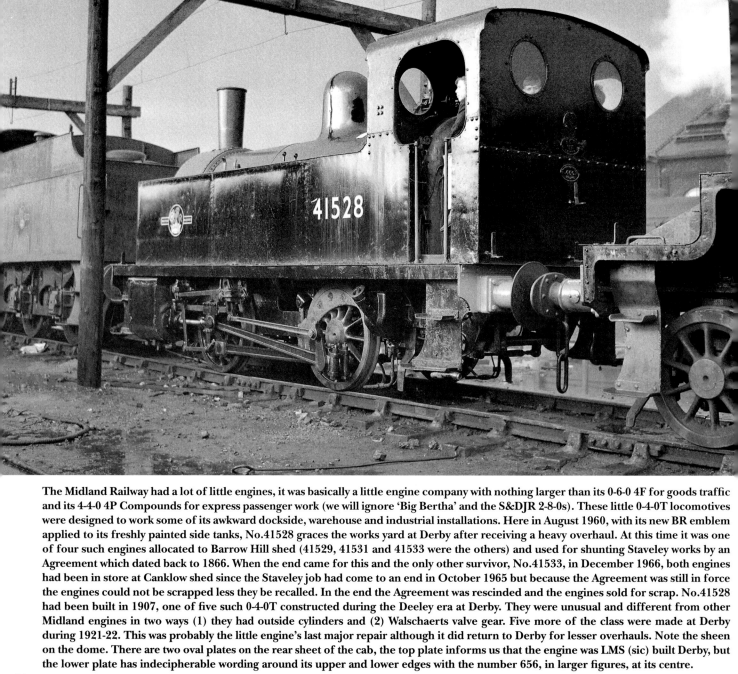

The Midland Railway had a lot of little engines, it was basically a little engine company with nothing larger than its 0-6-0 4F for goods traffic and its 4-4-0 4P Compounds for express passenger work (we will ignore 'Big Bertha' and the S&DJR 2-8-0s). These little 0-4-0T locomotives were designed to work some of its awkward dockside, warehouse and industrial installations. Here in August 1960, with its new BR emblem applied to its freshly painted side tanks, No.41528 graces the works yard at Derby after receiving a heavy overhaul. At this time it was one of four such engines allocated to Barrow Hill shed (41529, 41531 and 41533 were the others) and used for shunting Staveley works by an Agreement which dated back to 1866. When the end came for this and the only other survivor, No.41533, in December 1966, both engines had been in store at Canklow shed since the Staveley job had come to an end in October 1965 but because the Agreement was still in force the engines could not be scrapped less they be recalled. In the end the Agreement was rescinded and the engines sold for scrap. No.41528 had been built in 1907, one of five such 0-4-0T constructed during the Deeley era at Derby. They were unusual and different from other Midland engines in two ways (1) they had outside cylinders and (2) Walschaerts valve gear. Five more of the class were made at Derby during 1921-22. This was probably the little engine's last major repair although it did return to Derby for lesser overhauls. Note the sheen on the dome. There are two oval plates on the rear sheet of the cab, the top plate informs us that the engine was LMS (sic) built Derby, but the lower plate has indecipherable wording around its upper and lower edges with the number 656, in larger figures, at its centre.

Old meets new at Derby in August 1959. Johnson 1F No.41773 of 1890 vintage rubs shoulders with a fairly new Metro-Vick Co-Bo, the distinctive flush sides of which are unmistakable. During a short period in late 1959 all twenty of the Co-Bo fleet were allocated to 17A Derby when they first became operational on BR but by the end of that year eight of them had transferred to Cricklewood to start work on the 'shop window' CONDOR express freight service between London and Glasgow via the Midland main line. The Co-Bo locomotive type was the only one built for BR and in the end it was to prove to have been one of the numerous failures of the BR Modernisation Plan. By 1968 the class was deemed 'non-standard' and all except one example was condemned. That singleton, D5705, came back to Derby but was assigned to the newly set up Research Centre (where questions might have been asked as to why did BR purchase such rubbish in 1958 when perfectly good Standard 9F 2-10-0 .....!). Anyway, the unreliable bad boy of the early diesel era is now preserved but there are doubts as to its eventual return to main line running. Note the enthusiast with spectacles looking at the diesel hidden behind the 1F, he is scratching his neck and probably thinking 'What the !!!! next'. As for the half-cab 0-6-0T - well that was a Derby based, and built, engine which would keep going until the following summer when it attained the grand old age of seventy years and three months. Note 'Jinty' No.47315 in the background.

45

Although this picture is outside our date parameters, it is worth including simply because it shows a brand new Fowler designed 4F 0-6-0 which has just been turned out by Derby works in March 1939, some six years after Stanier had made his mark on the LMS. Of course, the LMS was not yet finished turning these engines out. After a lull of nearly nine years since the last batch had been put into traffic, by Crewe incidentally, the former LNWR workshop picked up the cudgel once again in May 1937 and produced another fifteen of these 0-6-0s. Not to be outdone Derby got in on the act in March 1939 and continued to grind out this, by now, ancient design for the next two years. Was it a lack of innovation or just desperation which contributed to the output of these locomotives in such numbers? Note that No.4578 has at least got a fairly modern high-sided tender (3500 gallons and 7 tons of coal).

Now here is a quick touch-up job if ever you have seen one. Johnson 1F half-cab No.41814 from Belle Vue shed was spotted at Derby shed on 31st May 1953 after a short visit to shops for, amongst other minor work, application of its BR crest which had replaced a very faded LMS, just about discernible on the tank side. It is recorded that this engine got its BR number in May 1950 but the bunker side number here appears to have been refreshed at least. Note the lamp irons on the platform are backed up by tall destination board brackets. Likewise the chunky lamp iron on the smokebox door has a destination board holder affixed behind it, which begs the question, when did this locomotive last run with destination boards? It was allocated to the Manchester shed throughout the BR period and for much of the LMS post-war period but prior to that, in 1935 at least, it was at Hasland shed. As far as is known this engine was never vacuum fitted and was built as a goods engine. The coupling are three-link and not screw type so where do these destination board brackets come into its history? It was withdrawn in March 1956 when its home depot was also closed. K.R.Pirt.

It hasn't had a full repaint, just a few touches here and there with the black brush but the exquisite lining, applied at an earlier works visit, still looks immaculate. This is Compound No.41116 in October 1953, on Derby shed after a visit to the nearby works. At this time the 4P 4-4-0 was working over the Cheshire Lines from Brunswick shed in Liverpool and would be engaged mainly on the express passenger services between Liverpool (Central) and Manchester (Central), a duty which would suit these large wheeled locomotives. The CLC sheds at Brunswick, Chester and Trafford Park had about twenty-five of the LMS built Compounds between them for running the fast passenger services from Manchester to Chester and the aforementioned route. K.R.Pirt.

Another nice lining job. This 2P, at Derby shed in August 1953, was a resident of 17A and had been since early LMS days but in June 1959 it was got rid off to Nottingham shed who withdrew it four months later - after little use. In the happier times of 1953 the engine was busy on the stopping passenger services radiating from Derby to Manchester, Sheffield, Nottingham, Lincoln, Leicester, Birmingham and Crewe. After two years rotting at Derby the 4-4-0 was finally purchased in October 1961 by local scrap metal merchant Albert Looms. Note the rack at leading in from the right; this was one of the radiating roads from the outside turntable.

Another type of locomotive synonymous with Derby was the Somerset & Dorset Joint Railway 2-8-0 tender engine class. Numbered 53800 to 53810 by British Railways, these Fowler designed locomotives worked for the whole of their lives pounding the Mendip hills, hauling both passenger and goods trains between Bath and Bournemouth. No.53801, seen at Derby in October 1953, was one of the original Derby built batch of six which were delivered to the Joint line in 1914 and numbered 80 to 85. In the summer of 1925 another five 2-8-0s (S&DJR Nos.86 to 90) were added to the fleet. These five were however built by an outside contractor, Robert Stephenson & Co. They were somewhat different to the Midland built engines in that they had larger diameter boilers, 5ft 3ins. against 4ft 9ins., and they had a left hand driving position. In 1930 the S&DJR locomotive fleet was absorbed into the LMS and the 2-8-0s were given new numbers (9670 to 9680) but those were changed in 1932 to become 13800 to 13810. All eleven engines were allocated to Bath Green Park engine shed (71G then 82F) and many remained active virtually until the line was closed although the first withdrawal took place in July 1959 when No.53800 went. No.53802 followed in March 1960 but after that the condemnation rate slowed down somewhat with two going in 1961, two in 1962, one at the end of 1963 and the remaining four between January and October 1964. Two of the 1925 built batch ended up being preserved on account that they had been purchased for scrap by a certain yard in south Wales. The others did get the chop with three going to another private yard, again in south Wales, but run by a very efficient Midlands based businessman. One engine ended up at Doncaster, four were scrapped at Crewe and only one, the class leader and first to be condemned was dealt with at Derby. No.53801 here was withdrawn in July 1961 and was one of the four sent to Crewe for cutting up. Note the automatic tablet catcher on the front of the tender, a requisite for working the Joint line. K.R.Pirt.

Remember the Stanier 3-cylinder 2-6-4 tank engines built for the London Tilbury & Southend line. Here is the last of the class No.42536 at Derby in August 1959, after it had undergone its final General overhaul. Numbered 42500 to 42536, these thirty-seven Cl.4 mixed traffic tank engines were the heaviest of all the LMS 2-6-4T, coming in at an all up weight of 92 tons 5 cwt. Although the main sphere of operation for the class was the LT&SR line, and they all ended up at either Shoeburyness or Tilbury, they were not adverse to working in other parts of the system, especially during LMS days and the list of depots which had their services is both geographically diverse and surprising. Nearer to their spiritual home was Cricklewood, Kentish Town, Watford and Willesden. A little further away but still in the Midland fold was Derby, Kirkby-in-Ashfield, Leicester and Nottingham. Going north again there was Lancaster, Manningham, Millhouses, Newton Heath, Normanton and Stourton. However, during 1951/52 a small number of them were tried out on the old South-western' lines in Scotland at Ardrossan, Corkerhill and Greenock Ladyburn before returning south to Plaistow. No.42536 started life at Trafford Park in December 1934 but moved over to Heaton Mersey in January 1935. Three months later it went, at last, to the LT&S line at Tilbury shed. During WW2 it was transferred away, first to Saltley in December 1942 then, in March 1943 Holbeck received it on board. It went back to Saltley in 1944 and finally back into the fold at Plaistow in July 1945. In October 1956 it was concentrated with most of the class at Shoeburyness from where it was withdrawn in June 1962. After a period of storage at 33C it was sent to Doncaster for scrapping in March 1963. Note that in this view the engine is still sporting a 33A Plaistow shedplate even though, officially, it was allocated to Shoeburyness.

When British Railways came into being, Rowsley engine shed was home to three of the former North London railway 0-6-0T which worked the Cromford & High Peak Railway. At that time Nos.27505 (58850), 27515 (58856) and 27530 (58862) were in residence. The rest of the class were either at home base, Devons Road which had six allocated or at Birkenhead, with half a dozen also, where their short wheelbase was found to be useful for working the docks there. No.58860 (ex 27527) was London based at the time (officially) but was actually working in Derbyshire on the C&HPR. This engine was an early recipient of a BR number and when applied in April 1948 it appeared in place of the LMS number alongside the legend LMS. In March 1955 it had come to Derby shed for some work or other to be carried out and by then the BR emblem was firmly in place with the number now positioned beneath. Note the chocks on either side of the centre coupled wheel. Was the work, whatever was required, to be undertaken out in the shed yard because it seems somebody did not want the engine moving? To the left an unidentified Compound has a NOT TO BE MOVED sign affixed but not the tank. Normally, during this early period of BR, these 0-6-0Ts would travel to their parent workshops at Bow for major repairs so the trip to Derby must have needed some urgent attention. The NLR tank was withdrawn in May 1957, it was fifth to last in the survival stakes. Three of the other four quickly followed, Nos.58856 (Rowsley) and 58859 (Devons Road) in November 1957 whilst No.58857, also Devons Road gave up in April 1958. Derby had by now taken responsibility for their upkeep at Bow works was all but closed. Nos.58856, 58859 and 58860 were all cut up at Derby whilst No.58857 was claimed by Crewe works, the connection there reaching way back to pre Titanic days. The lone survivor, No.58850 was still working on the C&HP line and although withdrawn in September 1960, it managed to become a candidate for preservation. Behind the tank is LMS Compound No.41192 which was minus its coupling rod.

Forward now to Derby shed on 29th August 1959, we see Hughes/Fowler 'Crab' No.42829 reversing down the yard whilst onlookers of all ages and sizes observe the fireman leaning out of the cab to make sure none of the visitors are getting in the way. Nowadays, the H&SE would probably put the 'mockers' on this kind of activity, i.e. leaning out of the cab so far. They would no doubt insist - order even that a flagman walk ahead of the engine to clear the road. Have we really come full circle from the 1830's? Besides the enthusiasts walking about the yard, there are at least seven of them at the top of the stairway on the side of the coaling plant. These people are of course having a grandstand view of the event below them and many had cameras too (we would like to see such views captured on film by readers, for inclusion in future albums). Back to the locomotive, this was one of the five Reidinger poppet valve engines which had originally been fitted, in 1931, with the Lenz rotary cam poppet valve gear. That early valve gear proved to be of no advantage given the expense so it was changed in 1953 for the Reidinger type, which also showed itself to be no better (it was a bad time for budding steam locomotion inventors). The five engines involved, Nos.42818, 42822, 42824, 42825 and 42829, all ended up at Burton-on-Trent depot (they had all been grouped at Saltley before that) and during May and June 1962 all five were withdrawn as their maintenance became untenable. 53

Alongside the shed on 28th November 1954 and obviously ex works was 4F 0-6-0 No.43886 with a distinguished lady for company and which had also been given a General overhaul. The 4F was one of Fowler's final 0-6-0 goods type developed for the Midland Railway and was put into traffic in 1919. It had a long lineage which would continue to be built at Derby, other LMS workshops and outside contractors up to and indeed into the first few years of World War Two. Even Crewe, the arch rival (enemy even) of the Derby 'type' built dozens of these engines through the LMS era. A Barrow Hill engine for most of its life, the 0-6-0 was withdrawn in October 1959 and after a period stored awaiting a buyer, it was taken to the Broughton Lane scrapyard of T.W.Ward in Sheffield, one of sixteen ex LMS 0-6-0s cut up at that yard. K.R.Pirt.

I don't know why but for some reason this picture, from that August 1959 Derby Works Open Day or Flower Show to give it its proper historical title, reminds me of the feature film Gremlins. But, thinking back, nobody, no matter how young, had a malicious or unsociable streak in them at these gatherings, at least nobody interested in railways. Therefore, the management felt quite happy to let thousands of people, many of them children, have the run of the premises and all that it beheld. Stanier Class 5 No.44863 had worked in from Rugby with an excursion bringing hundreds of enthusiasts to this event. I wonder how many more specials were run that day to bring people from far and wide? Exhibited engines included 'Britannia' No.70004 WILLIAM SHAKESPEARE, 9F No.92165, diesels 'Peak' D2 HELVELLYN, 0-6-0 DE shunter D3782, and Bo-Bo D5021. As a social observation, it would be interesting to know how much damage was caused, if any, by the public at these events. Events held during the days when people were given responsible for their own actions and for some reason were totally aware of that responsibility.

Yet another ex works locomotive on 28th November 1954. 'Jinty' No.47373 of Speke Junction makes a fine sight as it poses in the weak midday winter sun. Note the well patched tank sides which shows up well under the gloss black paint - still, never mind the grime will have it all covered again in a matter of weeks. This 0-6-0T was one of those which nearly made it to the end of steam and only missed out by about eighteen months but none of its class got as far as the end because the ubiquitous diesel shunters which became TOPS Class 08 had taken what little work there was for these shunting engines. Built by North British Locomotive Co. Ltd. in 1926, it was put into traffic during September of that year as LMS No.16456, it became 7373 under the 1934 renumbering scheme introduced at the start of the Stanier era to bring the whole LMS fleet into a reasonable, straightforward, uncomplicated numbering system. And it worked. No.47373 was one of those engines which got around its parent system and would seek work anywhere. By September 1935 it was at Chester, rubbing shoulders with the great Western engines which frequented that city. During the BR period it was still at 6A but had itchy tyres by 1950 and had moved across the Mersey to Speke Junction. In November 1955 it went north to Carnforth (if engines had intelligent and could see into the future you would have assumed by now that this 0-6-0T was on a mission to reconnoitre places to be when coming towards the end of steam). At the end of 1959 it transferred to Barrow but managed to get away from there during the following June, up the coast line to Workington. Six and a half years later, in December 1966, the inevitable took place - withdrawal. After an eight month period in storage the 3F tank was sold for scrap to J.McWilliams of Shettleston. Nearly forty-one years to the day the 0-6-0T had returned to its birth city.

K.R.Pirt.

Well what did you expect from an album based on Derby during the BR steam era? This is Johnson 3F No.43429 on 28th November 1954 fresh from the works and already at home. This 0-6-0 was a recent addition to the 17A Derby fleet having transferred from Coalville during the previous winter. This is yet another former Johnson Midland engine built in the Nineteenth century and still going strong. Constructed by Dubs & Co. in 1892, it was rebuilt subsequently by both Deeley and Fowler, receiving a Belpaire boiler from the last C.M.E. This engine transferred to nearby Rowsley in November 1955 and was finally withdrawn in April 1960. Doncaster works scrapped it during that summer. K.R.Pirt.

Even when they were filthy and unkempt, the LMS Compounds looked impressive, especially from a photographic angle such as this. Millhouses No.41190 was resting at Derby shed in May 1954 prior to working back to Sheffield. Built in March 1927 by Vulcan Foundry, this engine went to Bank Hall shed in Liverpool and was employed on various routes including Liverpool-Newcastle via Halifax, and the Liverpool-Manchester and Leeds services via Manchester and Halifax. After WW2 it transferred to Bolton shed (41103, 41104, 41189 and 41199 went too) where already it was under-utilised for its capabilities. But, the traffic to which it was used to, and built for, was no longer available to it; more modern motive power had taken over. In July 1952 it was sent to Grimesthorpe shed in Sheffield, a place hardly renowned for its express passenger locomotive stud and once again there was nothing for the 4-4-0 to do which was suitable. In September a move to Millhouses gave it a place amongst the passenger engine hierarchy in the city. Double heading heavy expresses became its lot for the next few years, with singleton workings to places like Derby, Nottingham and Leeds with semi-fasts. No doubt that is what brought it to Derby for this picture to be captured. In January 1958 it was realised that this engine, along with its surviving brethren, was living on borrowed time. Already some one hundred and forty of the class had been condemned since 1952 when withdrawals of the LMS engines began. In 1958 another thirty-six of the survivors would disappear leaving just nineteen. The last two LMS Compounds to work on BR were Nos.40936 and 41168, withdrawn in January and June 1961 respectively, and both of Monument Lane shed in Birmingham. It is ironic that this depot was ex London & North Western, a company which frowned upon compound working yet they were to harbour the last two icons of Midland Railway express passenger locomotives. Both these 4-4-0s had been in store at Monument Lane shed for some time, No.41168 since October 1958 for instance. No.41190 entered Derby works for the last time in January 1958 and never came out again.

In 1954 the LMS-built Compounds were still holding their own, withdrawals had started in 1952 but were still only running at about two a month, repairs were still taking place and a reasonable amount of double-heading of expresses was still in the offing. Bedford based No.41059 has just done some time in the shops and is ready to return to traffic on 28th of November along with another Derby built engine, Leicester based No.41097 which had likewise been through the works. In the event both engines did not have that much longer to work; No.41059 would disappear within a year whilst the Leicester engine would transfer to Nottingham and six months later, in May 1956, would face the chop. Note the middle cylinder steam pipe arrangement is different on each engine, one left, the other right. K.R.Pirt.

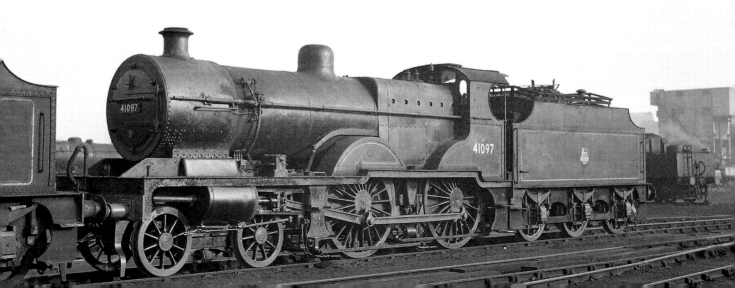

Three of the occupants of the dump at the timber sidings near Spondon junction in June 1959. 2P No.40534 is left but taking centre stage in this picture is Johnson half-cab 1F No.41661 complete with the new BR emblem and a new storm sheet bracket fabricated from coupling rods and other below footplate paraphernalia. It also has, on the rear of the bunker, just below the lamp iron, a brass? plate with the number 740 embossed as its centre. The periphery has an indecipherable legend top and bottom, each of one line. You can see one of the reasons why this engine was condemned by looking at the bottom rear edge of the bunker. No.41661's allocation history before withdrawal is quite interesting; in September 1935 it was shedded at Kentish Town along with eight more of the class. The north London depot remained home until July 1951 when it transferred to Grimesthorpe in Sheffield. Less than four months later it was in the clear air of Skipton but six months later it was drafted to Normanton, which although situated in the midst of the coalfields, still had some greenery about it in between the spoil tips, coke ovens and coal products plants. Next, in December 1955 it was back to city life for a while at Stourton. Finally, for its last two years of operational life, No.41661 was off to Goole to experience some chilling winds from the east. The withdrawal took place in June 1959 and as can be seen the 0-6-0t ended here in Turntable sidings at Chaddesden where it languished until October 1960 when it was towed the short distance to Looms yard at Spondon. Others listed amongst the Spondon junction gathering were: 40412, 40493, 40536, 40550, 41062, 41120, 41857, 43223, 43237, 43241, 43584, 43881, 43939, 47210, 47214, 49418, 58132, 58281. An ominous arrival here in November was Fowler 2-6-4T No.42341.

Doom and gloom at Chaddesden Turntable sidings in June 1959. LMS Compound No.41165 basks in the sunshine amidst a sea of grass, rust and assorted metals. Besides the 4-4-0 this dump contained at that time: 40538, 41795, 41878, 43253, 43292, 43324, 43355, 43369, 43506, 43629, 43651, 43930, 44369, 47216, 58085, 58178, 58308. As each week went by the rows were getting longer, even though engines were being pulled out for onward transit to private scrap yards.

Condensing 'Jinty' No.47216 hides another stored 'Jinty' at Chaddesden in June 1959. The yard here had been empty and derelict for some years before the arrival of the dead engines but prior to that happening, somebody went to a lot of trouble to check and replace all the rotten wooden chair keys so that derailments were kept to a minimum. No.47216 had not yet been condemned; it was August before inspections were carried out in earnest. It ended up at Looms yard just down the line. Although starting out when new at Bromsgrove shed, banking the Lickey incline, the 0-6-0T soon moved to London and then spent most of its life at Cricklewood shed. It would then have been 'shopped' at Bow works along with the other London based tank engines, visits to Derby were rare for these engines - no wonder they condemned them all the time!

Another section of Chaddesden's Turntable sidings in June 1959 with two generations of Midland 0-6-0 tender engines laid up alongside a woebegone 2P. Nearest the camera is 2F No.58167 of 1876 vintage, albeit rebuilt by the Midland after the turn of the century with a Belpaire boiler. Prior to BR numbering the engine in the 58114 series, this 0-6-0 carried the number 2994 until July 1952. in 1935 it was allocated to Westhouses shed moving coal trains down to Toton yard but at some time prior to WW2 it was sent to Saltley depot and worked from there until July 1956 when it transferred to Bournville after which it was down hill all the way to withdrawal. That was yet to happen but within a month the knives were out and this engine would be condemned in July. It was purchased by local scrap merchant Albert Looms and took the short journey to his yard at Spondon in September 1960. On the next line is 3F No.43210 (the perfect number backwards?) another Johnson design but built much later in 1890 by Neilson & Co. which also underwent rebuilding under Deeley. Note the much larger boiler compared with that carried by 58167. No.43210 still has its 21A Saltley shed plate adorning the smokebox door, no doubt someone was loathe to remove it after this engine had spent more than thirty years attached to that depot. This engine too was another which took the short one-way trip to Looms yard in September 1960. Note that both 0-6-0s have vacuum brakes and screw coupling.

From this angle the ex Midland 2P 4-4-0 looked pretty good, even in the surroundings of Chaddesden sidings in June 1959 it still appears majestic. No.40412 has suffered from a bit of accident damage to the front end, and is evenly covered with a thick coating of grime but nevertheless it still has an aura about it. Perhaps the presence of the ex LNWR 0-8-0 in front is adding to the illusion, the hard muscular appearance of No.49418, with its tender cab and small wheels says 'slow and lumbering' whilst the huge coupled wheels of No.40412 say 'swift and fleet of foot', the sound of them working hard was also impressive. No matter what we think of them now, or even then if we witnessed this gathering at first hand in June 1959, because these engines had no future before them. The 4-4-0 was built in 1892 by Sharp Stewart & Co. and, like all the old designs which got into LMS and later BR hands, they had at some point been extensively rebuilt from the original engine. This particular class not only got better boilers, with extended smokeboxes over the years, they also acquired new frames and a host of detail refinements which made them virtually into new engines. So, the true age of this locomotive would be nowhere near the 67 years the building date suggests, it was more like thirty-odd years after the Fowler rebuilding. Withdrawn in May 1959, this 4-4-0 had languished in Derby works, with sister engine No.40413, for some months before being condemned and then being brought to this dump but it was to end up in Looms yard during 1960. No.40412 had a varied career during LMS and BR days, being found at Buxton in 1935 then moving to Northampton before Nationalisation. It transferred to Upperby in July 1954 then in March 1957 it came back to its roots at 17A. What of the poor plodder? Well at this time the 0-8-0 was still officially operational and allocated to Stockport Edgeley shed (ex Nuneaton, Swansea and Northampton) so how and why it ended on Chaddesden dump is a mystery. It had apparently been here since June of the previous year and one can only assume that after working into Derby with a freight train it must have failed. It was eventually condemned but not until November 1959, however, being a product of Crewe, and knowing of the all time rivalry, animosity even, between the Derby and Crewe camps, the G2 was hauled over to Crewe works in March 1960 and cut up there.

Almost a 'Jinty' next to a real 'Jinty'. This is one of the rapidly diminishing breed of Johnson 1F 0-6-0T engines. The design was Johnson's first for the Midland Railway. Originally there was 240 of these useful engines within the class which had been built up between 1878 and 1899, and they became the standard shunting engine for the MR. An enlarged version of the class was introduced in 1899 and they became the first of the popular and numerous 'Jinty' design which in turn became the standard shunting tank of the LMS with over four hundred being built for the company between 1924 and 1931. Only ninety-five of the 1F design became BR property and No.41857 here carried a round-topped boiler until rebuilt in December 1954 with this Belpaire boiler. Built by Sharp Stewart & Co. in 1895, the engine came into traffic with the full cab unlike many of its class which had the half cab and which carried them to withdrawal in BR days (see illustrations of various engine numbered between 41660 and 41890 in this album). A long time resident of Grimesthorpe shed, withdrawal for No.41857 took place in May 1959 and it was purchased by one of the country's largest scrap merchants, T.W.Ward, who had the 0-6-0T hauled to their yard at Woodville, Burton-on-Trent in October 1960. The last examples of the class on BR were to be found stored at Canklow shed in 1966, ex Staveley works engines, and luckily one of them, half-cab No.41708 has been preserved. To the right is No.47214, from Cricklewood, which was withdrawn at the same time at 41857 but went just down the line for scrapping at Looms in August 1960.   65

Out of place? Certainly outnumbered but, in the end, not to be outdone, especially by these Midland upstarts. So might be the thinking if this ex London & North Western Railway G2 was animated. As eluded to elsewhere, this Stockport Edgeley based 0-8-0 found itself dumped at Chaddesden sidings after working into Derby, or perhaps Rowsley - the full story would be of interest - with a goods train and then failing in some way. It still has the 9B shedplate attached! Note that the Johnson 2F No.58132 behind the G2 has got a sack of sorts wrapped around the chimney rim denoting that it was at least stored serviceable. The date is June 1959 and the 0-6-0 had been condemned in May so the sackcloth is now superfluous and would only make a decent nest base for some of the winged inhabitants of this overgrown and derelict pasture.

(*opposite*) Four ex Lancashire & Yorkshire 2P 2-4-2Ts arrived at Albert Looms scrapyard in Spondon on the second day of June 1959. The hapless four were: 50818, 50831 and 50855 all from the Badnalls Wharf dump at Norton Bridge, and 50865 from Hillhouse shed in Huddersfield. This latter engine appears to be in a sound condition, certainly the paintwork and lining. Even the glass in the cab spectacles is unbroken, the whistle is still there and the cab fitting also seem to be intact. The engine has even got some coal on the cab roof left there from its last visit to the Hillhouse coaling plant. So that the buyer got every pound of metal for his pounds, the two pieces of the left hand coupling rod have been secured to the spring of the front radial. Note the temporary 'chock' beneath the front wheels has just managed to keep the engine on the rails. No.50865 had been around the L&Y system during its life, in 1935 it was resident at Newton Heath but on the eve of Nationalisation it was allocated to Southport after which it moved to Bolton. It transferred to Low Moor shed in July 1952 and then, in its first shift away from the parent system, it went to Huddersfield in September of that year. That was to be it final operational move. Withdrawn in October 1958, some eight months before it landed in Spondon, it truly is in a remarkable condition.

All of the 2-4-2Ts seem to have arrived at Looms yard with their coupling rods secured to the front springs. Perhaps it was a condition of sale, the rods being made of some of the more valuable metals. No.50818 has lost its chimney at some point during the period from leaving Sowerby Bridge, its last home, to arriving at Badnalls Wharf in November 1958 and the transit to Spondon. Looms yard, as can be seen, was not the tidiest and had whole and bits of wagons taking up the available space. Whatever happened to those smokebox numberplates, did they end up in a furnace or were they taken off and sold to enthusiasts? In September 1935 this engine was shedded at Carnforth but moved to Newton heath by wartime. Bolton shed was its next port of call in 1950 but it returned to 26A in April 1951. It preceded No.50865 to Low Moor by a month and worked from their for nearly to years before transferring to its final shed at Sowerby Bridge.

Sandwiched in between No.50818 and No.50855 was No.50831 which had been a native of Bolton since early LMS days and continued as such until July 1951 when it went to Lower Darwen. Eight months later it transferred to Lostock Hall but was there for just four months before crossing the border into Yorkshire and moving to Low Moor. Huddersfield had it for a year from late 1954 but it returned to Low Moor for a three year stint before it became a withdrawal statistic. Like No.50865 it appears in good condition considering the unsecured storage period out in the elements; the latter was helped perhaps by the Horwich paint shop which knew a thing or two about painting locomotives to face the elements.

This is No.50855 looking, for all intents and purposes as though it was having a rest whilst doing a spot of shunting. The wagon buffered up to the engine was a Western Region 21T Loco Coal wagon numbered W110481. Chalked over the black number square were the legends Stockingford and Looms - large un-missable COND tells the rest of its story. Before storage at Badnalls Wharf, No.50855 was another resident of Low Moor and travelled in convoy with the other two to Norton Bridge. On 23rd June these four early arrivals were joined by four more former L&YR 2-4-2Ts. Numerically they were 50646 from Bedford shed, 50725, 50757 and 50777 all from Badnalls Wharf. Although the dismantling at this yard was somewhat slow compared with what was to happen at other places in the not too distant future, two of the early June occupants had gone by the end of July.

Going forward in time now to 17th October 1964, to Chaddesden sidings but to look at a different batch of forlorn and unwanted hulks. 'Jubilees' now take up the siding space with Nos.45585, 45599, 45622 and 45723 languishing amongst the grass and weeds of this locomotive graveyard. No.45585, formerly HYDERABAD, had been resident at this dump from the previous May after being condemned at Derby shed, its home since January 1963. In November the nameless 4-6-0 was bought by T.W.Ward and taken to their Killamarsh yard near Sheffield. In front of the 'Jubilee' is 'Jinty' No.47320. Besides the 'namers' the other residents of the sidings on this day were Nos.42156, 44042, 44156, 45088, 47461 and J94 68013, ex Cromford & High Peak.

71

It seems strange that Nuneaton shed should have a 'Jubilee' allocated but in October 1961 four of them, Nos.45599, 45603, 45624 and 45669 were transferred there. In 1962 three more of the class joined them; Nos.45724 in July, 45723 in November and 45643 in December. No.45724 was condemned four months after its arrival and 45603 got the chop in December. Nothing more happened until the following February when Nos.45599 and 45723 went to work from Rugby. Both returned later to Nuneaton, 45599 in May 1963 and 45723 in July 1964. The former returning to Nuneaton when No.45669 had been withdrawn. For the next nine months the remaining 'Jubs' got on with it until Nos.45624 and 45643 departed in November - withdrawn. When No.45724 came back in July 1964 the end was 'on the cards' for the surviving pair and finally in August they were both condemned. Note that Nuneaton shed had tried to brighten up the front of No.45599 with a lick of paint here and there, as was the way at a lot of engine sheds at that time. Anyway, two of the Nuneaton seven were here at Chaddesden sidings on 17th October 1964 and both were destined to travel a little bit further afield before scrapping. No.45599 went to Cashmores at Great Bridge in November whilst No.45723 went as far as Birds at Swansea. Meanwhile at Looms, some five years after our last visit, that place was thriving and had the following awaiting attention: 43083, 44321, 45618, 47007, 49078, 84007 and 43110 being worked on.